CW00336491

THE ORIGINAL RULES OF RUGBY

FOREWORD BY MARTIN JOHNSON

INTRODUCTION BY JED SMITH

Bodleian Library
UNIVERSITY OF OXFORD

First published in 2007 by the Bodleian Library

Broad Street, Oxford OX1 3BG

Reprinted in 2009, 2010

www.bodleianbookshop.co.uk

ISBN: 1 85124 371 2

ISBN 13: 978 1 85124 371 6

Foreword © Martin Johnson

Introduction and this edition © Bodleian Library, University of Oxford

Images pp 44–5, 48–9 and 52–3 © Rugby School

Images pp 60–1, 64–5, 68–9, 72–3, 76–7, 80–1 and 84–5 © Museum of Rugby,
    Twickenham

All other images reproduced by kind permission of the Museum of Rugby,
    Twickenham

Designed by JCS Publishing Services, www.jcs-publishing.co.uk

Printed and bound in Croatia by Zrinski D.D.

A CIP record of this publication is available from the British Library

CONTENTS

FOREWORD

THE STORY OF A boy picking up the ball and running with it during a football match at Rugby School in 1823 created an enduring legend that would symbolise the game – and when England won the World Cup in Sydney in 2003, the trophy I held aloft was the Webb Ellis Cup, named after that same boy.

Rugby School laid the foundations of the game when they produced the first set of rules in 1845, and now the game is played worldwide and at a greater intensity than its founders could have imagined. The ethos of the game has undoubtedly changed. In the southern hemisphere in the 1980s and 1990s, rugby as I knew it was already professional in all but name in its standards of coaching, the nurturing of young talent, selection procedures, and the way the game was played. In order to compete, the home clubs had to follow this route, even if it meant dragging its administrators kicking and screaming towards the new era, and in 1995 the game became fully professional. As a result it is now harder, faster and ever more physical, but rugby remains a team game, at whatever level it's played, and the changing-room atmosphere and camaraderie before and after a game still prevail. There have been changes in the system but the rules, which embody the spirit of the game, still hold. Whether that spirit is still preserved is for individuals to judge, but those responsible should understand the game and have empathy with the players; to be effective, rules must be applied fairly and consistently.

It's unlikely that many players have ever studied the written rules reproduced here; they are something picked up on the field of play, sometimes the hard way! So this little book is a welcome and fascinating glimpse, for players and supporters alike, into the heart of the game they love.

INTRODUCTION

Why, you don't know the rules, you'll be a month learning them.
(East to Brown, *Tom Brown's School Days*, 1857)

'RUGBY HAS RULES? SERIOUSLY!!?' How many times has a first-time observer of the grand game been moved to utter such a comment on observing a rolling maul or a crushing tackle? Does even the hardened rugby supporter of either code (rugby union or rugby league) sometimes still catch themself wondering exactly what is going on before their eyes? A mud-splattered player wearing short trousers flies past the watching spectators, grasping on to an oval ball for dear life, avoiding the violent intentions of the opposition team and looking to throw the ball backwards so that it can ultimately be moved further forwards . . . Where on earth did it all come from?

Where it came from, in terms of its embryonic origins, is unknown to us and we are forced to employ historical sidesteps – phrases such as 'the mists of time'. We *do* know that for thousands of years, all over the world, robust free-for-alls involving the fight for possession of a ball between two warring teams has proved enduringly popular. Where it came from, in terms of the modern incarnation, is from the boys of Rugby School in Warwickshire. They gave it to the world and they did so via their rules of the game, first published in 1845.

To understand the evolution of rugby football and the importance of the 1845 rules it is also necessary to appreciate the evolution of rugby's great rival – soccer.

Association football (soccer) and rugby football did not magically emerge one day, fully formed and complete, blinking in the sunlight. The publication of the first rule books of the two major football codes were the result of a long, and sometimes painful, process. This process was initially played out in the public schools of England and then, in later years, the universities. The boys of the 'Sacred Seven' ancient medieval schools (Charterhouse, Eton, Harrow,

Rugby, Shrewsbury, Westminster and Winchester) played their own distinctive versions of the unruly medieval football games. The largely lawless 'folk football' games had often been played over huge distances with the objective being to take the ball over a parish boundary. The public school boys were playing within limited, and sometimes quite confined, spaces and so they had to construct precise rules for their 'football' games.

Individual circumstances necessitated local variations. The boys of Charterhouse, Harrow and the other schools were playing on cobbles, heavy mud or in narrow confines. These dictated that their versions of 'football' should be played standing up and with much of the physical confrontation removed. More emphasis was placed on ball dribbling or passing. At Rugby School, however, the wide expanse of grass on The Close allowed for a much more traditional version of 'football', where hacking, tripping, throttling and other more boisterous acts were common practice. It enabled the boys, in the absence of input or direction from any other quarters, to pursue an equally physical version of the ancient 'football' games – far more physical and confrontational than their contemporaries. Herein lay a key difference and the reason for the ultimate division between physical rugby football and the almost handling-free soccer. Had Rugby School not been blessed with a large expanse of grass, the physicality of the ancient football games could have been lost. The boys at Rugby School were refining an ancient legacy in their own image.

The versions of football played at Harrow, Charterhouse and elsewhere were eventually brought together in 1863, when the Football Association was formed with the intention of creating a set of 'compromise' rules so that supporters of particular school games could play against each other. Soccer was never intended as a separate game in itself, merely a way of allowing Eton boys to play against Winchester boys without the need for a prolonged and heated discussion before kick off on which rules to play by. Soccer was a compromise; practically a brand new version of 'football'. It was an attempt to call time on the endless arguments but was never intended to overshadow the rules of the venerable schools. Melvyn Bragg included the Football Association's First Rule Book in his *12 Books that Changed the World* and asserted in a sister publication to this that without the FA's 1863 Rule Book *"the game* [of soccer] *would never have been invented and the world would be a poorer place"*. Well, yes and no. The drive to play 'football' (in any guise or by any rules) was great and already growing beyond the schools. If the FA had not adopted and published their particular set of rules in 1863, then one of the other school rules (maybe even rugby football itself) or an alternative set of compromise rules could have easily filled the gap and satisfied the hordes.

So why is it that soccer is often (incorrectly) perceived as the ancient game, whilst rugby is seen as the wayward offspring? Step forward the attractive but misleading William Webb Ellis myth. This infamous story (boy picks up ball, runs with it and creates a brand new game) totally underplays the true origins and subtle evolution of the rugby game.

Ignoring the fact that there is not a shred of primary evidence to support it , there are two major problems with the myth. It is far more damaging than lovers of the tale would have us believe. To start with, because soccer has subsequently acquired sole ownership of the word 'football' in Britain, the myth's wording implies that Ellis was playing soccer at Rugby School. Not true. Rugby has far older traditions. Furthermore, another unfortunate result is that the genuine heroes of the rugby game's evolution have been sadly overlooked. They remain absolute unknowns in a game that otherwise cherishes its heritage and traditions.

Rugby School celebrates William Ellis, but the real story is that their own particular football rules prospered whilst numerous competitors failed. Only a few (The Eton field game, anyone?) are known beyond the confines of their birthplace. The truly revolutionary act at Rugby School was not the mythical William Ellis action. There was another act that enabled their game to survive, flourish and ultimately overshadow all competitors – the composition of the first ever written rules.

The 1845 laws (and their annually revised successors) were instrumental in the dispersion and survival of Rugby School's version of 'football'. They were the first written laws of *any* version of 'football'. However, the publication of the first rule book would, on its own, have been of little interest and minimal impact if there were not a great deal of interest in the goings-on at Rugby School beyond the stone walls that surrounded The Close. Two factors facilitated the spread of Rugby School's football game around the country and they are just as important as the published rules themselves.

The first was the influence of Dr Thomas Arnold's revolutionary educational model. Arnold was headmaster at Rugby School from 1828 until his sudden death in 1842, and whilst at the school he pioneered a very different approach to teaching. Prior to Arnold a Latin master would teach Latin. That was it. No other contact with the boys. No pastoral involvement in their growth, health or wellbeing. What Arnold wanted was to produce young men who were a combination of beast and monk – manliness and morality – and this meant greater involvement in the boys' lives. Closer supervision from his masters was encouraged so that waves of well-rounded, selfless, humble, 'muscular Christians' would be created.

Although he never directly encouraged or supported the boys' football games, Arnold's indirect impact on rugby football was enormous. The rugby pitch provided a perfect testing ground for the hardy, unselfish, fearless and self-controlled young men that Arnold wanted to produce – as part of a wider 'hardening' process. 'Football' also channelled the boys' aggression in an ordered way, to counterbalance their otherwise overly intellectual lifestyle.

The 'football' field was the arena where a boy's masculinity could be expressed and developed. Alongside the development of the rules of the game, a code of conduct and code of honour were also being produced. The game dovetailed perfectly with Arnold's educational model and so when Arnold's men (masters or old boys) left Rugby they took the game with them.

The unprecedented popularity of Arnold's educational model ensured that his masters were recruited to a wave of new public schools being created. Cheltenham, Marlborough, Wellington, Clifton and Haileybury were all founded within two decades during the mid nineteenth century. Having no football tradition of their own, they took to rugby football as readily as they took to Arnold's education model. Unlike other school games, rugby was expanding far beyond Warwickshire – providing a support network that would ultimately allow it to stand alone and survive once soccer started to dominate.

The other driving factor in the game's promotion was the popularity of Thomas Hughes' bestselling novel *Tom Brown's School Days*. Published in 1857, but set in the 1830s, it was incredibly successful. Within months 11,000 copies were on bookshelves in homes all over the country. Central to the book is the vivid depiction of the Rugby School football game, with young Tom as injured hero – celebrated by his contemporaries for a brave and courageous act on the football field. There is evidence that early clubs, such as the first club in Leeds, decided to play football by Rugby School rules, having read *Tom Brown's School Days*.

Arnold's educational revolution and Hughes' bestseller created a demand for the game beyond its birthplace, but it was a set of written rules that made the spread possible. So how did they develop?

Rugby School's peculiar version of 'football', with an oval ball, high goals, handling and large teams of unequal sides was already developed in the late eighteenth century, decades before the first laws were published. In the early years it seems to have been a very raw recreational activity with little need for hard

and fast laws. The boys would have been influenced by the various versions of 'folk football' that had been played in communities all over the country for many centuries: riotous, violent encounters; free-for-alls without rule or referee. The boys playing the game were picked from scratch, in ad hoc sides, and individual heroics were for the benefit of personal renown only and of little wider importance.

Arnold's requirement of a more ordered community in the school and his development of the house system changed everything. Playing against other houses or groups of old boys added a different dimension to the game. Boys were now heroes playing for the honour of their side – whether it was against rival boarding houses within the school, playing for the Sixth Form versus the rest of the school or for School House versus the rest of the school. Personal courage could now be demonstrated for the benefit of others – as encouraged in Dr Arnold's 'muscular Christian' model.

Laws were debated by the senior boys after each game on 'The Island', a Bronze Age mound within the school grounds. The younger boys learned the game whilst acting as goalkeepers, preventing the opposition from 'running in' (try scoring). It was whilst doing so that Tom Brown was winded in the novel's famous 'football' scene. Everyone was able to play the game at Rugby, sometimes in sides of hugely uneven numbers, in contrast to other schools where only limited numbers took part in 'football'.

When house honour was at stake, strict and enforceable rules suddenly had far greater currency and a rule book to resolve disputes was required.

The original 1845 laws were intended for those who already understood the game as played at Rugby School – not those who were new to it. The rules were a confirmation of the key hotly debated points of dispute at the time. They did not contain all of the rules, as these would have been well known to all Rugbeians, and so make for strange reading. There may have been another reason for the timing of the publication. The success of Arnold's educational model meant that increasing numbers of pupils were coming to Rugby. They would have been bringing 'outside' ideas to the football games, which necessitated the creation of written rules to aid the time-honoured tradition of handing down the rules by word of mouth and observation.

In 1844 the Head of School appointed a committee of eight boys to draw up the rules to ensure 'the better observance of football'. The following August the work was passed on to three senior pupils. The three pupils were William Delafield Arnold, the 17-year-old son of the former headmaster, W.W. Shirley, who was 16 years of age, and Frederick Hutchins. Within three days they submitted their 37 Rules to the Sixth Levee – the Sixth Form's decision-making body. They were immediately approved and it was agreed that a Rule Book be printed. No dissent was recorded so presumably the 37 Rules reflected the current laws exactly. The Rule Book itself was tiny so that it could be easily carried around – even onto the pitch itself.

The creation of the Rule Book was a Rugby School task and there was neither any intent nor comprehension that it might have any effect beyond The Close. Whilst cricket was played competitively against outsiders, football was an entirely internal affair. However, rules could now be disseminated around the country – to other schools looking to introduce a football game, to the old boys at the universities and to even older boys looking to set up the early clubs. If any Old Rugbeian wanted to return to school to play (as they were entitled to do) they needed to keep abreast of rule changes and updates. The records of the printer of the Rule Books show that one old boy alone ordered 50 copies of the 1847 rules – presumably for distribution beyond the school. This is the earliest evidence of dissemination.

The Rules themselves make for pretty difficult reading. After a preamble, intended to prevent anyone from skiving off matches, the 37 Rules themselves follow. Specific features on The Close at Rugby School are referenced, such as The Island and the three elm trees that stood within the field of play and could be used tactically to a team's advantage. The method of goal scoring (a conversion in modern parlance) following a player successfully running in (try scoring) is 'explained' in Rule 5. It was a very

convoluted procedure that involved punting the ball out from the place where the runner in went over the goal line, before another player attempted to kick for goal. Rule 6 tells us that games restarted with a place kick rather than a modern drop kick and the important role played by the school's prefects is referenced in Rule 35. Rule 31 mentions caps – the tasselled velvet caps awarded to the best players on the teams, and the origination of the practice of being awarded an international cap. Rules regarding offside and obstruction are familiar to us, whilst Rules 15 (no independent referees) and 20 (matches could last for up to five days – with breaks for sleep!) are a world away from the modern game.

The rules were updated regularly over the coming years by large committees who met annually to review and revise them but who usually only made a few necessary minor changes.

In 1862 a new approach was taken and an attempt was made to codify 'the customs' or full nature of the game as well as the laws, making dissemination even easier. It was the first manual for beginners, rather than pointers for existing practitioners. By now they were also being influenced by former boys as well, who wrote in requesting changes. It was not just universities and other schools that were asking for the rules but, by now, also the newly formed clubs such as Liverpool, Blackheath, Richmond and Sale. These 1862 rules are the link between the Rugby School rules of 1845 and the Rugby Football Union's first laws in 1871.

It was at this point in the story that the Football Association was created and rugby football (rather than being amalgamated) went its own way. Due to widespread interest in the game it was able to do so. The little law book had struck a significant victory.

The FA's first rules (in 1863) banned hacking. This was the divisive issue that drove supporters of Rugby School's 'football' away. They refused to play without an element of the game that was essential in developing character and manliness, through the ability to suffer pain with dignity. We can assume that the late Dr Arnold would have been delighted. Blackheath's Francis Campbell walked away from the FA and, in doing so, took rugby football with him. The irony that hacking is now the exclusive preserve of soccer players should not be overlooked!

The row about hacking did not end, however, despite the fact that by 1866 Blackheath and Richmond had both agreed to abandon it. It came to a head in 1870 in the pages of the national press after a player died in a practice match. The boys who had been happy to be hacked at school and had proudly flashed their hacking wounds like duelling scars were less willing to endanger their health and jobs as adults.

The Rugby School game was already well established by the 1870s through a mixture of good fortune and the missionary zeal of key individuals. Without a version of the standardised national rules that the FA had produced, clubs continued to develop variations of the Rugby School Rules, leading to difficulties when facing each other.

Benjamin Burns (Blackheath) and Edwin Ash (Richmond) wrote to *The Times* in late December 1870: "*. . . at present the majority* [of Rugby clubs] *have altered in some slight manner the game as played at Rugby School by introducing new rules of their own.*"

The rules of the home side were traditionally employed, putting the opposition at a great disadvantage. Sometimes half of a match was played by one set of rules and half by another. This was a traditional way of resolving disputes in many early games of 'football' and is the origin of the concept of halftime. It was also difficult to implement Rugby School's rules on regulated pitches when they were framed with specific reference to the boys playing on The Close at Rugby.

On 26 January 1871, the Rugby Football Union (RFU) was founded in the Pall Mall Restaurant in London, to standardise the rules and also remove some of the more violent aspects of the Rugby School game. Thirty-two men met, representing 19 clubs and two schools. Rugby School was notable by its absence. The boys there had always been unwilling to hand control of their game to school masters, so were even less likely to hand it over to a foreign body.

So, ironically, the Rugby School game was finally codified without direct involvement by the school and, in a sense, 1871 was a defeat for the school. They finally lost control of their game through a desire to maintain the independence that the 1845 Rules had been published to achieve.

Along with the founding of the Rugby Football Union, a committee was formed, and three ex-Rugby

School pupils (Algernon Rutter, Edward Holmes and Leonard Maton) were invited to help formulate a set of rules. The three were players at Richmond and Wimbledon Hornets and, being lawyers, they formulated 'laws' not 'rules'. As in 1845 it was a three-man sub-committee who did the work and much of the terminology derived from those original Rugby School rules. Maton took on the majority of the work – being housebound with a broken leg. This task was completed and approved by June 1871 and it is very likely that the laws were drawn up in Maton's home in Wimbledon.

Unfortunately (for anyone English) the new laws were not composed in time to be employed at the very first international rugby match: Scotland versus England in Edinburgh. As was customary, the home side's version of the laws were utilised and the Scots emerged victorious. The English team's overnight journey to Scotland on hard wooden benches in third-class accommodation would not have helped either.

The greatest irony was that the RFU's 59 original laws of 1871 finally banned hacking (Law 57) – the very issue that had prevented rugby from being swallowed up into the FA in 1863. The practice was formally abolished at Rugby School itself in 1876.

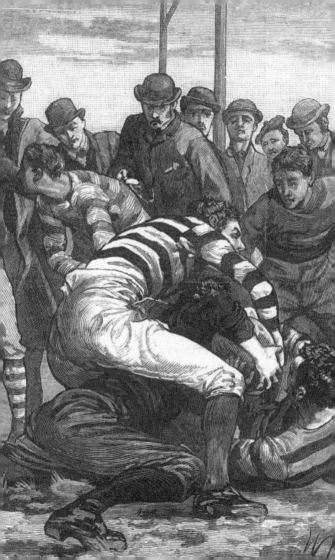

Of the 59 RFU laws of 1871, broadly 50 per cent are still current. There were only slight changes made to Rugby School laws of the period – such as prohibition of hacking – and such changes were designed to speed up and simplify the game. Although many concepts remain alien to us, it is a far more recognisable game than that described (in heavily abridged form) in 1845.

Law 6 reminds us that a field goal (kicking the ball over the bar, off the ground whilst it is bouncing around during open play) was allowed – and would remain permitted until 1905. Law 11 describes the scrum of the period – a prolonged, upright, shoving and kicking session, featuring as many players as happened to be in the immediate vicinity when it was formed. Laws 19 and 20 remind us of the struggle for possession once a ball crossed the try line – a reference back to the enormous rolling mauls that composed the early games at Rugby School. Law 15 is evidence that 'running in' was still the preferred term for try scoring, whilst Law 18 explains that a tackled player is forced to place the ball on the floor – far closer to modern rugby league's 'play the ball' rule than modern rugby union's rucks and mauls.

Law 26 is the first sign of the pass from hand to hand, player to player, although it would be another

20 years before the concept of passing for tactical advantage was considered a useful move, rather than a coward's way of avoiding punishment if caught with the ball. Law 28 tells us that a fair catch (a modern 'mark') could be made anywhere on the pitch, and a goal could be scored from a mark. Law 32 outlines three different ways to return the ball to play from touch – one of which is the modern line-out. The place kick (not drop kick) still restarted games, whilst Law 38 suggests that it was common for sides to change ends after every goal was scored.

A less convoluted goal-scoring method than that listed in 1845 is offered in Law 47 – the origin of the current try-scoring/converting law. However, the more complex 1845 version was still permitted (Laws 29, 46, 48, 49, etc. . . .). That it was still necessary to articulate Law 58 implies that the game retained its ultra-violent traits, even though hacking was now finally banned. Finally, Law 59 reminds us that independent arbitrators were still not involved in the game, a situation that would not change until the 1880s.

The Laws would continue to develop and of as much interest as the Laws themselves are those that are absent. Team sizes were not mentioned in the Laws until 1892 – having been reduced from 20 to

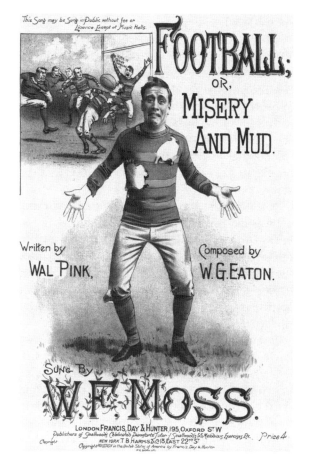

This Song may be Sung in Public without fee or Licence Except at Music Halls.

FOOTBALL;
OR,
MISERY
AND MUD.

Written by
WAL PINK,

Composed by
W. G. EATON.

SUNG BY
W. F. MOSS.

LONDON, FRANCIS, DAY & HUNTER, 195, OXFORD ST W
Publishers of Smallwood's Celebrated Pianoforte Tutor / Smallwood's 55 Melodious Exercises Etc.
NEW YORK T B HARMS & C 18, EAST 22ND ST
Copyright MDCCCXCV in the United States of America by Francis Day & Hunter

Price 4

the modern 15 by common consent in the mid 1870s. The dimensions of the field were first regulated in 1879, the size of the ball in 1892 and the duration of the match (incredibly!) not until 1926. These aspects continued to be regulated by tradition and habit rather than through the Laws.

The 1871 Laws marked the point at which Rugby School's game of football became the international sport of rugby football. It was these laws that would, on the back of empire, spread the game around the globe.

In the end the RFU themselves would lose control of the game. By 1890 the RFU had been forced by the Rugby Unions of Scotland, Ireland and Wales to join the International Rugby Football Board (IRFB, now the IRB). The English contingent initially had a power of veto on the IRB, holding as many seats as the other participating nations combined, but they no longer wielded ultimate power over the game.

Just as the senior boys had sat on The Island at Rugby School after each game discussing the laws, so the laws of rugby (now framed by the IRB) continue to evolve. They reflect the dynamic, professional sport that rugby union has become. It is a tradition of innovation that has served the game well. A similar flexibility has been absent in soccer where the difficulty of scoring goals (and the likelihood of drawn games) means that the random lottery of the bolted-on penalty shootout frequently decides cup competitions and league titles.

Rugby School's 1845 'football' laws did not mark the origin of one sport, however, but of many. The giveaway clues are the oval balls and upright posts that can be seen all over the globe. On Australia's eastern seaboard, 'football' means rugby league – a 13-a-side variant of rugby that developed in northern England in the late nineteenth and early twentieth centuries after a schism within the RFU. In other large swathes of Australia, 'football' means Australian rules – a game codified in 1859 by a group of young men including Tom Wills. Wills had been sent to Rugby School only a few years after the publication of the school's original 1845 Rules. In North America 'football' means American football – another game which developed directly out of rugby. These variations have given pleasure to countless millions of people around the world, derived from one shared ancestry.

Over-complexity in the laws has, admittedly, always been rugby's greatest weakness, especially when compared with the 'jumpers-for-goalposts' simplicity of soccer. But once the rules are understood, complexity ceases to remain a disadvantage. How many people would really prefer a game of draughts over a game of chess?

Like many legends, rugby's own of tale of William Ellis is wonderfully simple and therefore enduring. But when you see the Rugby World Cup trophy (which is named in his honour) being handed over to the captain of the best rugby team on the planet, remember the roll call of rugby's less glamorous heroes: Dr Thomas Arnold, Thomas Hughes, William Delafield Arnold, W.W. Shirley, Frederick Hutchins, Francis Campbell, Benjamin Burns, Edwin

Ash, Algernon Rutter, Edward Holmes and Leonard Maton. These were rugby's true heroes. All of them, in their own way, promoted and spread the rules of 'football' as played at Rugby School. These are the written rules that turned a school game into a global sporting phenomenon.

Jed Smith
Museum of Rugby, Twickenham

THE LAWS OF
FOOTBALL AS PLAYED
AT RUGBY SCHOOL
28TH AUGUST 1845

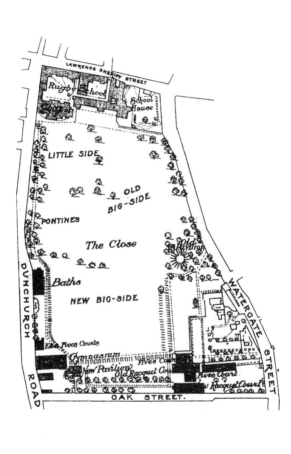

RESOLUTIONS

That only in cases of extreme emergency, and only by the permission of the heads of the sides, shall any one be permitted to leave the Close, after calling over, till the game be finished, and consequently, that all dressing take place before that time.

That the punishment for absenting oneself from a match, without any real and well-grounded reason, be left to the discretion of any praepostor. That whenever a match is going to be played, the school shall be informed of it by the Head of School in such a manner as he shall think fit, some time before dinner on the day in question.

That no unnecessary delay take place in the commencement of the matches, but as soon as calling over be finished, the game be commenced. That the old custom, that no more than two matches take place in the same week, be strictly adhered to, of which, one must always take place on Saturday, without some strong cause to the contrary.

That all fellows not following up be strictly prohibited from playing any game in goal, or otherwise conducting themselves in any way which shall be deemed prejudicial to the interests of their side.

That in consequence of the great abuse in the system of giving notes to excuse fagging, &c. and otherwise exempt fellows from attendance at the matches, no notes shall be received which are not signed by one of the Medical officers of the school and countersigned by the Head of House or by a master when the case specified is not illness.

That all fellows at Tutor during calling over, or otherwise absent, shall be obliged to attend as soon after as possible.

That the Head of School take care that these resolutions be generally known among the school, and as far as the case may be they shall apply equally to the big sides.

That Old Rugbeians shall be allowed to play at matches of Football, not without the consent, however, of the two heads of the sides.

RULES

1. FAIR CATCH is a catch direct from the foot.

2. OFF SIDE. A player is *off his side* if the ball has touched one of his own side behind him, until the other side touch it.

3. FIRST OF HIS SIDE is the player nearest the ball on his side.

4. A KNOCK ON, as distinguished from a *throw on*, consists in striking the ball on with the arm or hand.

5. TRY AT GOAL. A ball touched between the goalposts may be brought up to either of them, but not between. The ball when *punted* must be within, when caught without, the line of goal: the ball must be place-kicked and not dropped even though it touch two hands and it must

The following football-[...]
School, by receiving the [...]

1. Fair catch is a catch direc[...]
2. Off Side. A player is Off [...]
one of his own side behind [...]
3. First of his Side is the plac[...]
4. A knock on, as distinguished [...]
the ball on with the arm or [...]
5. Try at Goal. A ball tou[...]
up to either of them, but n[...]
be within, when caught, w[...]
be place-kicked & not dro[...]
& it must go over the ba[...]
touched the dress of any play[...]

became the ~~~~~ of

~~~ of the Sixth.

~ the foot.

~de, if the ball has touched
~~~, until the other side touch,
~rest the ball on his side.
~ a throw on, consists in strikin~
~d.

~ between the Goal Posts may be ~~
~tween. The ball, when punted, ~~
the line of Goal; the ball m~~
even when it touch two hands~
between the Posts without having
the person. No Goal may be

go over the bar and between the posts without having touched the dress or person of any player. No goal may be kicked from touch.

6. KICK OFF FROM MIDDLE must be a place-kick.

7. KICK OUT must not be from more than ten yards out of goal if a place-kick, not more then twenty-five yards, if a punt, drop, or knock on.

8. RUNNING IN is allowed to any player on his side, provided he does not take the ball off the ground, or take it through touch.

9. CHARGING is fair, in case of a place-kick, as soon as the ball has touched the ground; in case of a kick from a catch, as soon as the player's foot has left the ground, and not before.

10. OFF SIDE. No player being off his side shall kick the ball in any case whatever.

11. No player being off his side shall hack, charge, run in, touch the ball in goal, or interrupt a catch.

12. A player being off his side having a fair catch is entitled to a fair *knock on*, and in no other case.

13. A player being off his side shall not touch the ball on the ground, except in touch.

as the players' foot has le[ft]

10. No player being off his side

whatever.

11. No player being off his side

the ball in goal, or inter[?]

12. A player, when off his o[wn]

of a fair knock on; o[r]

13. A player, being off his

the ground except in tou[ch]

14. A player, being off his s[ide]

player on his side, by [?]

15. Touch. A player may r[un?]

in or this Touch.

the ground, & not by

all kick the ball in any case

ll hack; charge; run in; touch

a catch.

having a fair catch. is entitled

no other case.

shall not touch the ball on

cannot himself or any other

ing or throwing on the ball.

any case run with the ball

14. A player being off his side cannot put on his side himself, or any other player, by knocking or throwing on the ball.

15. TOUCH. A player may not in any case run with the ball in or through touch.

16. A player standing up to another may hold one arm only, but may hack him or knock the ball out of his hand if he attempts to kick it, or go beyond the line of touch.

17. No agreement between two players to send the ball *straight out* shall be allowed on big-side.

18. A player having touched the ball straight for a tree, and touched the tree with it, may drop from either side if he can, but the opposite side may oblige him to go to his own side of the tree.

19. A player touching the ball off his side must *throw* it *straight out.*

20. All matches are drawn after five days, but after three if no goal has been kicked.

21. Two big-side balls must always be in the Close during a match or big-side.

22. The discretion of sending into goals rests with the heads of sides or houses.

23. No football shall be played between the goals till the Sixth match.

24. Heads of sides, or two deputies appointed by them, are the sole arbiters of all disputes.

25. No strangers, in any match, may have a place-kick at goal.

26. No hacking with the heel, or above the knee, is fair.

27. No player but the first on his side, may be hacked, except in a *scrummage*.

28. No player may wear projecting nails or iron plates on the heels or soles of his shoes or boots.

29. No player may take the ball out of the Close.

18. A player, having touched
the ball with it, may drop
opposite side may oblige

19. A player, touching the ball
it straight out.

20. All matches are drawn if
goal be kicked.

21. Two big-side balls must
match or big-side.

22. The direction of sending
sides & Houses. *

23. No Foot-ball shall be
with Match.

24. Heads of Sides, or two

ball straight for a line, standing
either side. if he can. but the
go this one side of the line.
his side in back. must throw

v days; but after 111. if a

be in the Close during a

goal nets with the heads of

between the Goals before the

appointed by them are the

30. No player may stop the ball with anything but his own person.

31. Nobody may wear cap or jersey without leave from the head of his house.

32. At a big-side, the two players highest in the School shall toss up.

33. The Island is all in goal.

34. At little-sides the goals shall be four paces wide, and in kicking a goal the ball must pass out of the reach of any player present.

35. Three Praepostors constitute a big-side.

36. If a player take a punt when he is not entitled to it, the opposite side may take a punt or drop, without running if the ball has not touched two hands.

37. No player may be held, unless he is himself holding the ball.

As these Rules have now become the Laws of the game, it is hoped that all who take an interest in Football will contribute all in their power to enforce their observance.

— 1871 —

RUGBY FOOTBALL
UNION.

Proposed Laws

OF THE

Game.

E Carleton Holmes & Son
12 Bedford Row
WC

Plan of the Field.

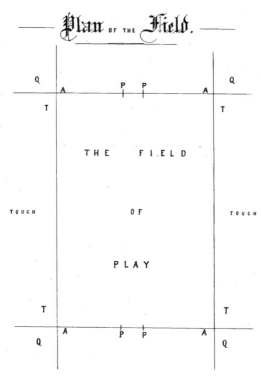

AA . AA . *Goal Lines* PP . PP . *Goal Posts*
TT . TT . *Touch Lines* QQ . QQ . *Touch in Goal*

The Touch lines and Goal lines should be cut out of the Turf

THE LAWS OF
THE GAME OF
FOOTBALL AS PLAYED
BY THE
RUGBY FOOTBALL
UNION

The following is an attempt to present the final draft as approved on 22 June 1871 by the Committee, and on 24 June by a Special General Meeting

1. A *drop kick* or *drop* is made by letting the ball fall from the hands and kicking it at the very instant it rises.

2. A *place kick* or *place* is made by kicking the ball after it has been placed in a nick made in the ground for the purpose of keeping it at rest.

1.   A '<u>Drop Kick</u>' or 'dro

fall from the hands and

rises.

2.   A '<u>place kick</u>' or '<u>place</u>'

after, it has been placed i

the purpose of keeping it a

3   A '<u>punt</u>' is made by

hands and kicking it 'b

made by letting the ball

ing it the 'very instant' it

Cap^{tn}

Cap Tn

Cap Tn

de by kicking the ball in

ick made in the ground for

t.

g the ball fall from the

3. A *punt* is made by letting the ball fall from the hands and kicking it *before* it touches the ground.

4. *Each goal* shall be composed of two upright posts exceeding 11 ft in height from the ground and placed 18 ft 6 inches apart with a cross bar 10 ft from the ground.

5. A *goal* can only be obtained by kicking the ball from the Field of Play direct (i.e. without touching the dress or person of any player of either side) over the cross bar of the opponents' goal whether it touch such cross bar or posts or not: but if the ball goes directly over either of the *goal posts* it is called a *poster* and is not a goal.

6. A goal may be obtained from any kind of kick except a *punt*.

7. A match shall be decided only by a majority of goals.

8. The ball is dead when it rests absolutely motionless on the ground.

9. A *touch down* is when a player putting his hand upon the ball on the ground in touch or in goal stops it so that it remains dead *or fairly so*.

10. A *tackle* is when the holder of the ball is held by one or more players of the opposite side.

11. A *scrummage* takes place when the holder of the ball being in the field of play puts it down on the ground in front of him and all who have closed round on their respective sides endeavour to push their opponents back and by kicking the ball to drive it in the direction of the opposite goal line.

12. A player may take up the ball whenever it is rolling or bounding except in a scrummage.

13. It is not lawful to take up the ball when dead (except in order to bring it out after it has been touched down in touch or in goal) for any purpose whatever – whenever the ball shall have been so unlawfully taken up it shall at once be brought back to where it was so taken up and there put down.

the ball shall have been

at once be brought back to

there put down.

14   In a scrummage it

with the hand under an

15   It is lawful for any,

with it, and if he does

purpose whatever – whenever

unlawfully taken up it shall

it was so taken up and

lawful to touch the Ball

cumstance whatever

er who has the ball to run

is called 'a run'. If a playe

14. In a scrummage it is not lawful to touch the ball with the hand under any circumstances whatever.

15. It is lawful for any player who has the ball to run with it, and if he does so it is called a *run* – if a player runs with the ball until he gets behind his opponents' goal line and there touches it down, it is called a *run in*.

16. It is lawful to *run in* anywhere across the goal line.

17. The goal line is in goal and the touch line is in touch.

18. In the event of any player holding or running with the ball being tackled and the ball being fairly held he must at once cry *down* and there put it down.

19. A *maul in goal* is when the holder of the ball is tackled inside the goal line or being tackled immediately outside is carried or pushed across it and he or the opposite side or both endeavour to touch the ball down.

20. In case of a maul in goal those players only who are touching the ball with their hands when it crosses the goal line may continue in the maul in goal and when a player has once released his hold of the ball after it is inside the goal line he may not again join in the maul and if he attempts to do so may be dragged out by the opposite side. But if a player when *running in* is tackled inside the goal line then only the player who first tackled him or if two or more tackle him simultaneously they only may join in the maul.

21. *Touch in goal* (see plan). Immediately the ball whether in the hands of a player (except for the purpose of punt out see Rule 29) or not goes into touch in goal it is at once dead and out of the game of and is brought out as provided by Rules 41 and 42.

22. Every player is *on side* but is put *off side* if he enters a scrummage from his opponents' side or being in a scrummage gets in front of the ball, or when the ball has been kicked, touched or is being run with by any of his own side behind him (i.e. between himself and his own goal line).

outside is carried or push

side or both endeavour

the Ball is ~~in touched~~ down it shall

and ~~bylep~~ the, ~~he~~ gained

20 In case of a maul,

are touching the ball

the goal line may conte

when a player has once

after it is inside the g

across it and he or the opposite

uch the ball down (See Back
ng to side in whose side it is for touched down
speion of the Ball ~

oal those players only who

their hands when it crosses

in the maul in goal and

eased his hold of the ball

ne he may not again join

23. Every player when *off side* is out of the game and shall not touch the ball in any case whatever, either in or out of touch or goal, or in any way interrupt or obstruct any player, until he is again *on side*.

24. A player being *off side* is put *on side* when the ball has been run five yards with or kicked by or has touched the dress or person of any player of the opposite side or when one of his own side has run in front of him.

25. When a player has the ball none of his opponents who at the time are off side may commence or attempt to run, tackle or otherwise interrupt such player until he has run five yards.

26. *Throwing back*. It is lawful for any player who has the ball to throw it back towards his own goal, or to pass it back to any player of his own side who is at the time behind him in accordance with the rules of *on side*.

27. *Knocking on* i.e. deliberately hitting the ball with the hand and *throwing forward* i.e. throwing the ball in the direction of the opponents' goal

line are not lawful, and in either case the captain of the opposite side may require [inferred: the player to bring it back to the place of the infringement] and there put it down.

26 'Throwing back': It is ...

the ball to throw it back ...

it back to any player. of ...

time behind him in accor...

27 'Knocking on', i.e. delib...

hand and 'Throwing forw...

~~and in either case it ~~may~~ shall the~~

direction of the opponents ...

~~the captain of the opposite~~

~~the ball be either knocked~~

28 A 'Fair Catch' is a ca...

ful for any player) who has

vards his own goal, or to pass

own side who is at the

ce with the rules of on side

ly hitting the ball with the

' i.e. throwing the ball in the

of the opposite may umpire

and then but it down

f line are not lawful. If

less, a fair catch has been made

or thrown forward. The Captain of the

made direct ^ from a kick

28. A *fair catch* is a catch made *direct* from a kick or a throw forward or *knock on* by one of the opponents' side, or from a punt out or a punt on (see Rules 29 and 30) provided the catcher makes a mark with his heel at the spot where he has made the catch and no other of his own side touch the ball.

29. *A punt out* is *a punt* made after a touch down by a player from behind his opponents' goal line and from touch in goal if necessary towards his own side who must stand outside the goal line and endeavour to make a fair catch or to get the ball and *run in* or *drop* a goal. See also Rules 49 and 51.

30. A *punt on* is a punt made in a manner similar to a punt out and from touch if necessary by player who has made a fair catch from a *punt out* or another *punt on*.

31. *Touch* (see plan). If the ball goes into touch the first player on his side who touches it down must bring it to the spot where it crossed the touch line, or if a player when running with the ball cross or put any part of either foot across the

touch line, he must return with the ball to the spot where the line was so crossed, and from thence return it into play as follows.

32. He must then himself or by one of his own side, either *i)* bound it out in the field of play and then run with it, kick it or throw it back to his own side or *ii)* throw it out at right angles to the touch line or *iii)* walk out with it at right angles to the touchline any distance not less than five or more than 15 yards and there put it down first declaring how far he intends to walk out.

33. If two or more players holding the ball are pushed into touch the ball shall belong in touch to the player who first had hold of it when in the field of play and has not released his hold of it.

34. If the ball when thrown out of touch be not thrown out at right angles to the touch line the captain of either side may at once claim to have it thrown out again.

35. A catch made when the ball is thrown out of touch is not a *fair catch*.

either foot across the to

& from thence return it in

Ball to the spot where

32 either case must himself

bound it out in the Field

kick it or throw it back

it out at right angles

with it at right angles

ine he must return with the

fieldy Msay or ~~provided by the follows~~

line was so crossed, ~~and on~~

one of his own side, either *i.*

Play and then run with it

his own side or *ii* throw

touch line or *iii* walk out

touch line any distance not

36. *Kick off* is a place kick from the centre of the field of play and cannot count as a goal. The opposite side must stand at least 10 yards in front of the ball until it has been kicked.

37. The ball shall be *kicked off i)* at the commence-
    ment of the game *ii)* after a goal has been
    obtained.

38. The sides shall change goals as often as and
    whenever a goal is obtained unless it has been
    otherwise agreed by the captains before the
    commencement of the match.

39. The captains of the respective sides shall toss up
    before the commencement of the match, the
    winner of the toss shall have the option of goals
    or the kick off .

40. Whenever a goal shall have been obtained the
    side that has lost the goal shall then kick off.

41. *Kick out* is a drop kick by one of the players of
    the side which has had to touch the ball down
    in their own goal or into whose touch in goal the
    ball has gone (Rule 21) and is the mode of bring-
    ing the ball again into play, and cannot count as
    a goal.

42. *Kick out* must be a *drop kick* and from not more
    than 25 yards outside the kicker's goal line. If

it has been kicked.

37   The Ball shall be ~~k~~

the game – ii ~~after change~~

ii

~~Rule 37 iii~~ after a goal

38   The sides shall char

~~as often~~ as and

~~iz, upon the expiration~~

as often as a goal has bee

~~upon for the duration of~~

speed by

~~– the Captains before the~~

off ; at the commencement of

~~roals as provided by the next~~

been obtained

~~roals are only drawing a ment~~
never b. a fral is oblained
~~half the whole time agreed~~
~~Noined~~   N. has been
~~made unless by the Agreement~~

~~sap as often as and wherever~~

the ball when kicked out pitch in touch it must be taken back and kicked out again. The kicker's side must be behind the ball when kicked out.

43. A player who has made and claimed a fair catch shall thereupon either take a *drop kick* or a *punt* or *place* the ball for a *place kick*.

44. After a fair catch has been made the opposite side may come up to the catcher's mark and (except in cases under Rule 50) the catcher's side retiring, the ball shall be kicked from such mark or from a spot any distance in a direct line (not being in touch) behind it.

45. A player may touch the ball down in his own goal at any time.

46. A side having touched the ball down in their opponents' goal, shall *try at goal* either by a place kick or a punt out.

47. If a *try at goal* be made by a *place kick* a player of the side who has touched the ball down shall bring it up to the goal line subject to Rule 48 in a straight line from and opposite to the spot where

the ball was touched down and there make a mark on the goal line and then walk straight out with it at right angles to the goal line such distance as he thinks proper and there place it for another of his side to kick. The kicker's side must be behind the ball when it is kicked, and the opposite side must remain behind their goal line until the ball has been placed on the ground (see Rules 54 and 55).

48. If the ball has been touched down between the goal posts, it may be brought out in a straight line from either of such posts but if brought out from between them the opposite may charge at once (see Rule 54).

49. If the *try at goal* be by a *punt out* (see Rule 29) a player of the side which has touched the ball down shall bring it straight up to the goal line opposite to the spot where it was touched down and there make a mark on the goal line and then *punt out* from any spot behind the goal line not nearer to the goal post than such mark, or from touch in goal if necessary, beyond which mark it is not lawful for the opposite side who must keep behind their goal line to pass until ball has been kicked (see Rules 54 and 55).

47 If the ball has been

may
posts. it ~~must~~ be brough

either of such posts but
~~Case the~~ ~~opposite~~ ~~any~~ chan

49 If the 'try at goal' l

a player of the side

shall bring it straight

spot where it was touch

...hed down between the goal

...t in a straight line from

~~taught back~~
from between them ~~to which~~
~~Rules~~ at once (see rule 5.4)

...1 a 'punt out' (see Rule 29)

...o has, touched the ball down

...o the goal line opposite to th...

...own and there make a mark on

...any spot behind the goal line by

50. If a fair catch be made from a *punt out* or a *punt on* the catcher may either proceed as provided by Rules 43 and 44 or himself take a *punt on* in which case the mark made on making a fair catch shall be regarded (for the purpose of determining as well the position of the player who makes the *punt on* as of the other players of both sides) as the mark made on the goal line in the case of a *punt out*.

51. A catch made in touch from a *punt out* or a *punt on* is not a fair catch: the ball must then be taken or thrown out of touch as provided by Rule 32 but if the catch be made in touch in goal the ball is at once dead and must be *kicked out* as provided by Rule 21.

52. When the ball has been touched down in the opponents' goal none of the side in whose goal it has been so touched down shall touch it or in any way displace it or interfere with the player of the other side who may be taking it up or out.

53. The ball is dead whenever a goal has been obtained, but if a *try at goal* be not successful the kick shall be considered as only an ordinary kick in the course of the game.

54. *Charging* i.e. rushing forward to kick the ball or tackle a player, is lawful for the opposite side in all cases of a place kick after a fair catch or upon a *try at goal* immediately the ball touches or is placed on the ground; and in cases of a drop kick or punt after a fair catch as soon as the player having the ball commences to run or offers to kick or the ball has touched the ground but he may always draw back and unless he has dropped the ball or actually touched it with his foot they must again retire to his mark (see Rule 56). The opposite side in the case of a punt out or a punt on, and the kicker's side in *all* cases may not charge until the ball has been kicked.

55. If a player having the ball when about to *punt it out* goes out side the goal line or when about to *punt on* advances nearer to his own goal line than his mark made on making the fair catch, or if after the ball has been touched down in the opponents' goal or a fair catch has been made, more than one player on the side which has so touched it down or made the fair catch, touch the ball before it is again kicked the opposite side may charge at once.

56. In cases of a fair catch the opposite side may come up to and stand anywhere on or behind a line drawn through the mark made by the player who has made the catch and parallel to their own goal line; but in the case of a fair catch from a *punt out* or a *punt on* they may not advance further in the direction of the touch line nearest to such mark than a line drawn through such mark to their goal line and parallel to such touch line. In all cases (except a punt out and a punt on) the kicker's side must be behind the ball when it is kicked but may not charge until it has been kicked.

57. No hacking or hacking over or tripping up shall be allowed under any circumstances.

58. No one wearing projecting nails, iron plates or gutta percha on any part of his boots or shoes shall be allowed to play in a match.

59. The captains of the respective sides shall be the sole arbiters of all disputes.